Contents

KW-053-690

Introduction

Most of us take family life for granted. Everyone has a mother and a father! However, not all of us live with them. Here we look at the many types of family in Britain today. Is the family changing and why? Should we allow the stereotype of the perfect family – Mother, Father and two children – to continue? Does the breakdown of family life lead to crime and violence? Statistics show that one in three to four marriages now ends in divorce, so many of us will face changes in our home life which may make us feel helpless and vulnerable. This book helps explain how family life is affected by the changes in society and gives us more understanding of our own and other people's families.

What makes a family?

Mr Bun

the Baker

Mrs Bun

the Baker

Master Bun

the Baker's Son

Miss Bun

the Baker's Daughter

The word family often means different things to different people. All over the world people are living in family groups but how they do so depends on many factors, such as their country and culture, or religious beliefs.

This book considers the concept of the family from a westerner's point of view. Whether you live in India or Iceland , your idea of a family will be influenced by your own experience. If you live in the western world some of the ideas on these pages may well have influenced you.

This definition of a family reinforces the idea that a family is made up of people who have married and had children.

This is a family set from the game 'Happy Families'. All the family sets show a man with a profession, his wife as assistant and their son and daughter. This familiar portrayal of the family can make a strong impression on us and **stereotype** the image of a family.

The family way

Most societies rely on the family to 'reproduce, nurture and socialize'. This means that families are required to make sure that we are born and survive, and that we are cared for and taught how to behave with others. Government surveys show that marriage and family life is the way most people live.

1960s DEFINITION

FAMILY, group of persons related by blood and marriage; group of parents and children; children of same parents

FACT

In Britain, 95% of women and 91% of men choose to marry by the time they are 49. Statistically, the average couple will have 2.4 children.

FAMILIES

Andrea Willson

Heinemann
LIBRARY

H www.heinemann.co.uk

Visit our website to find out more information about **Heinemann Library** books.

To order:
- ☎ Phone 44 (0) 1865 888066
- 📄 Send a fax to 44 (0) 1865 314091
- 💻 Visit the Heinemann Bookshop at www.heinemann.co.uk to browse our catalogue and order online.

First published in Great Britain by Heinemann Library, Halley Court, Jordan Hill, Oxford OX2 8EJ, a division of Reed Educational and Professional Publishing Ltd.
Heinemann is a registered trademark of Reed Educational & Professional Publishing Limited.

OXFORD MELBOURNE AUCKLAND
JOHANNESBURG BLANTYRE GABORONE
IBADAN PORTSMOUTH NH (USA) CHICAGO

Designed by Tinstar Design (www.tinstar.co.uk)
Illustrations by Oxford Illustrators
Originated by Ambassador Litho Ltd
Printed by Wing King Tong in Hong Kong

ISBN 0 431 03531 8 (hardback)   ISBN 0 431 03536 9 (paperback)
04 03 02 01 00   04 03 02 01 00
10 9 8 7 6 5 4 3 2   10 9 8 7 6 5 4 3 2 1

British Library Cataloguing in Publication Data

Willson, Andrea
    Families. – (What's at issue)
    1. Family – Juvenile literature 2. Teenagers – Family relationships – Juvenile literature
    I. Title
    306.8'5

Acknowledgements

The Publishers would like to thank the following for permission to reproduce photographs:
Advertising Archives p 5; Bubbles/ Hercules Robinson p 41,/Loisjoy Thurston p 8,/Bruno Zarri p 37; Trevor Clifford pp 4, 38; Hulton Getty p 6; Gingerbread p 13; Sally Greenhill pp 11, 20; The Stockmarket p 42,/Ariel Skelley p 31; Tony Stone Images/Elie Bernager p 16,/Walter Hodges p 17,/ Bruce Ayres p 27,/Josh Pulman p 34; Trip/Chris Simpson p 19.

Cover photograph reproduced with permission of Trevor Clifford Photography.

Our thanks to Julie Turner (School Counsellor, Banbury School, Oxfordshire) for her comments in the preparation of this book.

The author would like to thank John Asher of Cumbria County Council Social Services; Edna Callanan, the Librarian at Ulverston Victoria High School; Katherine May of Parent-Link; the helpful staff at Barrow Health Promotion Unit and everyone else who has helped with information and support in writing this book.

For Joey and the students of Ulverston Victoria High School.

Any words appearing in the text in bold, **like this**, are explained in the Glossary.

This advertisement from the 1950s and the more recent 'OXO' advertisement show that there has not been much change in people's image of what a typical family is.

> Shirley Hughes is a popular British children's author whose stories focus on another happy family.
>
> 'Grandma had a big book of pictures. There were photographs of everyone in the family. Alfie liked looking at them with her and asking who all the different people were … there was a picture of Mum and Dad at the seaside, before they got married. There were some pictures of Alfie and Annie Rose, too, when they were tiny babies. The one Alfie liked best was a picture of himself having a bath in the old baby bathtub.'
>
> from *Grandma's Pictures* by Shirley Hughes

Family life usually provides more than the essentials needed for survival – it provides security, love and comfort, too. These can make it a great source of happiness, which is why it is a popular choice of lifestyle. But influential images like the 'cornflakes' family suggest you have to be a member of a certain kind of family in order to be happy.

The nostalgic view

Nostalgia means looking back into the past and believing that things were better then. For example, some people believe that family life was better when parents had traditional roles and always stayed together. However, when people are nostalgic they often forget the bad things and only remember the good, and this can make them feel dissatisfied with the present and suspicious of change.

The idealistic view

When we have an idea of what is perfect or right and try to achieve it but can't, we feel as if we have failed. We become unhappy with what we have actually got. Some people suffer because their family life doesn't follow the **stereotypical** image.

This book looks at how people's ideas of family life have developed, what family life is actually like today, and what might be the typical family of the future.

5

Families in the past

Family life is always influenced by practical circumstances. Although many families still suffer financial hardship, generally our society is much better off materially today than in the past.

Problems in the past

In the past, most families were affected by other **pressures** as well as poverty. These pressures remained for hundreds of years.

- Most families were large because of a lack of **contraception** and poor understanding of family planning. Couples tended to marry, or form partnerships, and start having children while they were very young.
- A limited understanding of medicine and **nutrition** meant that life expectancy was shorter and children often died young, so it was common for families to experience serious illness and death.
- There was no **welfare system** so families depended upon each other for support. Many families sent their children out to work as soon as possible. Illness meant a serious loss of earnings and often the loss of a job.

For all except the well-off, the home was probably cramped, insanitary and damp. Food was very basic and there was not much of it, so health was poor. Wealthier families fared better, but because there was little knowledge of nutrition and disease, not even the rich could rely on good health.

In the past it was very hard to change your circumstances. Education was a privilege for the wealthy, and girls were only educated to be good wives and mothers.

> Attitudes to marriage have influenced family life for hundreds of years. This quotation from an ancient text on Welsh law shows that people tolerated divorce in medieval times.
>
> 'husband and wife can part for adultery or some lesser causes – and if a woman leaves a husband "for leprosy, and for lack of **marital relations**, and foul breath" she does not even lose her dowry.'
>
> from *The Medieval Idea of Marriage*, by Christopher Brooke

For poor people in 1917 a good home meant strong emotional bonds rather than material comforts.

Modern times

The twentieth century has brought new influences which have had a dramatic effect on the family:

Cause	Effect
Men fought in wars and often died. In **WW1** most families lost at least one male relative	*Women went out to work*
After **WW2** families were invited from overseas to help economies in countries such as Great Britain	*A multicultural society developed*
Great Britain became more prosperous and education became a right, not a luxury	*People had more leisure time and knowledge*
Better medicines, vaccinations and methods of family planning became available	*People had longer, healthier lives*
More personal freedom became available	*The divorce rate increased*
The **welfare state** offered security and support to the poor	*There was less dependence on the family*

Personal freedom

Our modern society now emphasizes the rights of the individual. Many people recall a childhood or marriage which they would have been glad to escape if there had been more personal freedom. In the past, the head of the family was usually the man, and the wife and children had to live according to his wishes.

In Victorian times, the wealthier and better educated tried to impose their views on how poor families should live.

'Poor though the labourers might be… they would learn to save when times were good…The women would keep their dwellings neat and clean, learn to budget and cook nourishing meals, control their children, send them to school (and to Sunday school), and assist the authorities by reporting infectious disease or infestation. The men would actively look for paid work and not drink their earnings away. Children would attend school and go out to work. They would contribute to the family coffers and, when they left home, maintain their parents in need. These features added up to respectability and responsibility.'

from *Family Tree to Family History*, by Ruth Finnegan & Michael Drake

Travel

Some older people claim that families and communities are not as close as they used to be. This may be partly due to the ease with which people can now travel. In the past, a trip to a nearby town meant you either walked or went by horse, so people travelled less and spent more time at home. People can now easily commute to work every day. In the past, people used to spend their whole lives in the area where they were born. Today many choose to live elsewhere, and may even move to another country.

The changing family

One thing never changes – people will always seek happiness through their relationships with others. Our closest relationships are with our family, but perhaps now more than ever before the word 'family' means many different things to different people.

Families now

This father takes care of his daughter while her mother goes out to work.

FACT

*The **stereotypical** image of a family as a working father, mother at home and 2 children accounts for only 5% of families in Britain today. So what makes up the other 95%? Do they conform to the traditional views on family life?*

1995 DEFINITION

Surprisingly, modern dictionary definitions hardly differ from those of a hundred years ago.

FAMILY, one's **spouse** and children; one's children; group descended from a common **ancestor**; group of related beings

Families today take many different forms, including single-parent families, step families, extended families, foster families, adoptive families, families with two Mothers, families with two Fathers and grandparent families. The traditional view of the family is being affected by certain changes in society and in people's attitudes.

Modern trends

WORKING WOMEN: women have fought hard for equality. They only gained the right to vote in Britain in 1918. Now women have more rights, which mean they are able to plan a career and family. Today approximately 33 per cent of families have mothers who go out to work. This has affected the role of both men and women in the home.

DIVORCE: in 1995 there were 155,499 divorces in Britain. Increasing rates of divorce and remarriage have lead to rising numbers of families with single parents or new parents who are not blood-related to the children.

GAY RIGHTS: it is no longer illegal to be **homosexual**. From 1967 adults over 21 could 'share homosexual practices in private'. In 1994 the age of consent in Britain was lowered to 18 years. These changes in the law and in attitudes towards sexuality have meant that more homosexuals feel able to live with partners of the same sex. Also, **heterosexual** couples are breaking up because one partner wishes to live with someone of their own sex.

MULTICULTURAL SOCIETY: many people have moved to live in other countries of the world. As a result, societies have become more **multicultural**. For example, people who have moved to Britain have brought their own traditions with them, such as religious beliefs and ways of living. Their views on family life influence the existing views of people around them.

ADOPTION: the modern trend in adoption is to place children in racially similar families. Although, some couples sometimes adopt children from other

I should be allowed to express my own views freely.

I should not be deprived of health care as a standard of living adequate for my spiritual, moral and social development.

parts of the world, especially when children have been orphaned by conflict.

Rights of the individual

All these social changes seem to reflect the increasing importance of people's personal rights in modern society. This is reflected in the **Universal Declaration of Human Rights**, some of which is quoted below:

'Adults have the right to marry and found a family regardless of race or religion'.

'Both men and women are entitled to equal rights within marriage and in divorce'.

Children's rights have increased, too, which means they now have more say in how they wish to be treated.

Responsibility to others

Having one's own rights means having to respect other people's rights, too. Modern family members may need to do some careful juggling so that they can find personal happiness without becoming selfish. Selfishness can threaten the happiness of the whole family.

The nuclear family

A **nuclear family** consists of parents and children. Nuclear means 'the centre point' and a nuclear family is the centre point of a larger group of relatives who live elsewhere. The relatives who live apart from the central family group may be part of another nuclear family.

FACT

46% of the population live in a household with dependent children aged between 0–18 years. Of these, 75% have married couples as parents, and 6% have co-habiting parents.

My Dad can't get a job.

My Mum earns more money than my Dad. They both work because they both want to. When I was little I went to a childminder.

My Mum and Dad are always arguing about who does what at home but neither of them want to give up work.

The nuclear family is still the most common type of group living together in Britain. Is this by choice or does it just happen?

Changing roles

In the past the roles of the father and mother in a nuclear family were well defined. Each knew what was expected of them and whether they were personally fulfilled or not was unimportant. This has now changed.

More choices

Couples now have far more choices in how they live their lives together. This offers more personal freedom and opportunities for fulfilment and material comfort. But it now seems more important than ever that they agree on the practicalities of raising a family. There are no longer any clear rules by which to live.

For many different reasons, some couples are now choosing to live together but not get married. This is called co-habiting. To enter into marriage with vows and promises seems to suggest commitment and stability to those who choose to get married, and are unnecessary formalities to those who don't. The law still **discriminates** between married and unmarried couples.

What's in a name?

Married or not, some couples are now choosing not to use the man's surname as a family name because this discriminates against women. Step-family members also bring new surnames into a family. A surname no longer always identifies a child with his or her parents.

THE LAW

INHERITANCE: if a couple co-habit and one partner dies, the surviving partner does not automatically become a beneficiary. If a couple are married, the surviving partner does.

DIVORCE: if a co-habiting couple separate, neither partner has the automatic legal rights to the other's assets. If a married couple divorce, a legal procedure takes place to share the assets.

CHILDREN: if a couple are unmarried and have children, the father does not automatically have parental responsibility for any offspring. This means that they do not have any automatic rights either. If married, both parents have equal rights to the children.

I've got my Mum's surname. My brother's got my Dad's.

We've got a double-barrelled name.

Mum and Dad say I can choose which surname I have when I'm older.

I've got my Mum's name as a middle name. My Mum has kept her maiden name and calls herself Ms. She says it's nobody's business whether she's married or not.

I've changed my name to my step-Dad's name when my Mum got remarried.

Children, career or both?

By 1993 one in five of all mothers in Britain with children under 16 were working full-time, and two in five were working part-time. Yet surveys suggest that women still take the main responsibility for household chores.

Parents and children today face many compromises if they are to be successful members of a nuclear family, and not just survivors.

Some fathers and mothers have swapped traditional roles but the majority of working mothers still balance their careers with the care of their children.

11

One-parent families

Not all children live with both parents. A household in which there is a lone parent with a dependent child (or children) is called a one-parent family.

One-parent families occur for a variety of reasons: the loss of a parent through illness or accident; a woman decides that she wants to bring up a baby alone; a teenage girl becomes pregnant and isn't supported by the father of the child; or a couple split up.

Family support

When a family experiences a separation, divorce or death, a period of bereavement usually follows. However, while society acknowledges the effects of a death in the family and offers support, society often only criticizes, judges or blames parents when a divorce, unplanned pregnancy or separation happens. As a result, the parents can be left with the feelings of failure and shame.

A modern phenomenon

In Britain, statistics show that the main reason for the increase in one-parent families is due to the fact that, since the 1970s, there has been an increase in broken marriages. This does not actually mean that more people have been unhappy in their relationships. Instead, it reflects a change in the law. In 1971, the Divorce Reform Act made divorce easier, so couples who may have previously found it difficult to separate were able to do so from the 1970s onwards.

One-parent families can find advantages in their situation. If the divorced parent is happier than before there will be less tension and fewer arguments in the home. Child-parent bonding may become stronger, and household organization simpler. A parent's new life may lead to more life choices.

Lone needn't mean lonely

Many lone parents struggle with the pressures of bringing up their children without support and having to fulfil the roles of both father and mother. There are groups where single parents can come together and share their feelings, and often, a single-parent may find another partner.

Practical arrangements

In the past, when a couple split, the mother usually kept the children. However, as the roles of parents have changed this, too, has changed. The parent who looks after the children (has **custody**) is often decided legally through the courts. The courts decide according to what is best for the children's future financial care and control.

Often, a period of adjustment will cause financial difficulties which may take some time to overcome. Many single parents suffer financially because they are the only or main provider for the children. However, many separated parents become good friends and are able to raise their children more harmoniously when apart than when living together.

Parents and children at a social event run by Gingerbread – an organization created so single parents can meet and share experiences.

It was awful when my parents split up. At first I thought I was going to crack up. But now I can see they're so much happier and I feel better than if they'd just stayed together for my sake.

When Mary died, I wanted to die too. But I had to keep going for the kids' sakes. They've been brilliant and now I feel closer to them than ever before.

Too many people give up at the first sign of trouble. You've got to try and make it work for the sake of the children. After all, it's them that suffer most.

FACTS

The length of time spent as a single parent can vary from a few weeks to a lifetime and it seems that the majority of lone parents are women.

- *1 in 3 marriages will end in divorce*
- *1 in 8 families is headed by a lone parent*
- *1 in 9 lone parents is a father*
- *1 in 7 is an unmarried mother*
- *1 in 6 is a **widowed** mother*
- *1 in 3 is a divorced mother*
- *1 in 5 is a separated mother*

My Mum says she feels really sorry for some of her friends whose husbands drive them crazy.

I feel guilty about my Mum and Dad splitting up. If I hadn't been born they would never have argued so much about money and stuff.

13

Step families

A step family is a family that is related by remarriage, not by blood. Today, step families are called **reconstituted** families. This suggests something that has been put back together to make it whole again. It mainly refers to the changes that take place when couples with children find new partners.

New partners

If, or when, a single parent finds a new partner and they decide to marry or live together, the family becomes 'reconstituted'. Naturally, the dynamics of the family will be affected. Dynamics are the exchange of feelings and responses to people and situations. The arrival of a new partner may fulfil the adult's needs. But children have needs too and these have to be approached in different ways.

Figure 1: a. shows the ideal, and b. the possible reality. But unfortunately human nature means that life is often not so simple, see c.

1a

Oh goody! I'm so glad Mum has found herself such a great boyfriend.

Me too! He's great isn't he? He treats us like adults and he earns loads of dosh!

He read me a bedtime story last night and he said that he loves us as much as he loves Mummy.

1b

He's so cool. My friends are dead envious. He makes their dads look boring.

Do you think Daddy minds?

No! He says he can't imagine anyone nicer being our step-dad.

1c

What's he doing here again? I thought Mum said this was our family day.

Mummy said we should try to get on with him better because we're going to be seeing a lot more of him.

But Daddy said that Sue's got too much to do now with the new baby.

If he moves in, I'm moving out!

Back to Dad's of course!

Yeah! But look at her! She can't keep her hands off him! She's got no time for us any more.

But where will you go?

Dad, Mum, I hate them both! Where are we in all this?

Michelle is beautiful. I haven't felt like this about anyone since I split up with Jayne. They're nice kids, although that Naomi can be a bit of a handful, and Michelle spoils the boy. I wonder if she loves them more than she loves me? Oh well, I suppose I'll soon get used to them. I hope Jayne finds someone soon. I can't afford to support two families.

I deserve some happiness, too. The kids will soon get used to Kev. He's great with his own kids, and mine need a father who's there for them all the time – not just every other weekend!

Why can't Mum just be happy with us? I mean, she can have boyfriends but why do they have to move in? We get on great on our own and Mum's a different person when she's not with a man. That Kev is a pain. I don't trust him at all. I bet he starts treating her badly once he gets what he wants.

Why do we have to pretend it's working out?

I miss Daddy. Everybody has changed. I want it to be how it used to be.

Figure 2: There's also Dad and Sue and Jayne, and Kev and Jayne's children, plus the grandparents, friends, neighbours and society in general who all have their own thoughts and opinions on whether Mum should let Kev move in with her and her children. Understanding others can be difficult because we easily become selfish when our happiness is threatened. Sometimes it helps to try and imagine what others are feeling.

There are endless implications in such a situation as this. It's not difficult to see how a loving home can be turned into a battlefield of confused emotions. Everyone involved needs care and consideration if they are to survive the changes without being damaged. Some people say that damage to the individual is inevitable in the break-up of a marriage, but with better understanding it can be minimal.

Although there seem to be numerous problems, reconstituted families do succeed. They can provide advantages such as more family relatives, happier parents and more secure children. If the adults recognize that children do not divorce their parents and the children can see that their parents may well form new attachments, then a changed situation can work out. Also, there are support groups to help every family member. With care and thoughtfulness we are more likely to lose the **stereotypical** image of the wicked step-parent and replace it with a friendlier image.

Alternative families

Some families don't fit any particular label, yet they are definitely family groups (adults caring for dependent children).

In Britain, many children live with relatives other than their parents. The reasons can vary – their parents may have died or be unable to look after their children. In such cases if an able relative, or friend of the family, wishes to become a **legal guardian** then they are viewed favourably by the **welfare system**.

Grandparents

Sometimes grandparents find themselves in the roles of parents to their grandchildren. This can offer a new lease of life to the grandparents, and the grandchildren may experience much love and devotion. However, an older generation who may have been looking forward to retirement and a quieter lifestyle may suddenly have to adapt to the pace, demands and costs of a younger generation! Having brought up their own children, now they must care for their children's children! The children may have to adapt and learn to understand that their grandparents cannot do the things their parents did. Some families adapt and cope with these **pressures**, often finding that their lives are affected in a positive way. Others may find the changes difficult and frustrating.

In some cases the legal guardian or godparent of a child may have to fulfil their promises to care for a child.

Other relatives

Other relatives who become parents face similar difficulties. Aunts and uncles will probably feel a deep bond with the children of a brother or sister, but they will still have to cope with the changes involved in taking the role of parent. In these situations the main needs of a child are to feel wanted and loved. Some children have to take a place in an existing family and may feel like an intruder. The carer could feel resentful of the extra responsibilities. However, with understanding and reassurance, usually these problems can be overcome.

It is a common tradition to appoint guardians or godparents for a child. This ensures that if anything should happen to the parents, there will be adults appointed by the parents who have promised to care for the child.

A new lease of life or just more work? These grandparents have taken on the responsibility of looking after and caring for their grandchildren.

Gay partnerships

'As a child from an alternative family, I can assure everybody that it is love that counts and not two married parents. My mother, sisters and our gay, male role models were the envy of those of my friends who were tired of hearing their parents fight.

A gay/**lesbian**/single-parent family is one that requires extraordinary thought and commitment on the part of the parents. People who are willing to fight for their families surely send the most important messages to their children – that they are valued.'

Ron Elliott, York

from *The Guardian* 'Letters to the Editor' 7 November 1998

Government and the family

This letter above was sent in response to a controversy raised by a new British government document in the autumn of 1998 which encouraged the nation to live in nuclear family units. The government assessed 'family values' as those which are mainly found within **nuclear family** units. It stated that many of society's problems stem from the breakdown of traditional family life.

Having two Mothers or two Fathers

Many gay couples want family life just as much as 'straight' couples. Increasingly, they are making their feelings heard in a society that struggles to deal with its **prejudices** and moral uncertainties.

The Media

Television, and the media generally, reflect our changing attitudes and our responses to what is regarded by many as 'different'. Over recent years the media has given more coverage to gay issues and people are speaking more openly about their experiences of **homosexual** relationships.

In an article in a popular women's magazine, Nikki O'Reilly talks openly about living in an all-female household with her mother and lesbian partner, Lois:

'When she [Lois] first moved in I gave her a bit of a hard time – I was jealous and used to having my Mum to myself. Apparently, I would look at whatever food she was cooking and say, "Urgh. What's that muck?" But I soon got used to having her around and called her Flommy (a cross between father and mummy) from very early on. Sometimes Mother's Day would become an issue and we'd have a separate Flommy's Day but I never felt as if I was missing out, as the good always outweighed the bad. It wasn't just that they were good in comparison – they were also supportive and intelligent. They gave me a lot of confidence in myself which I think a lot of parents fail to do. They knew they were breaking the cycle of traditional parenting, and that they would have to challenge people's prejudices, so they thought, "Right, how are we going to bring this kid up?" My Mum believed that children should be happy and loved and allowed to express themselves.'

Nikki O'Reilly

from *Marie Claire, 1998*

Newspapers sometimes take a viewpoint that is less sympathetic:

> 'Dawn Whiting and Lisa Dawson are living apart, their dream of lesbian domesticity in tatters. The couple, who used sperm from different **donors** to **inseminate** each other, provoked outrage when the story of their children was first revealed.
>
> They insisted they could provide a secure, long-term home and even exchanged vows and rings in a "marriage" ceremony. Now, however, 22-year-old Miss Whiting is understood to have found a new female partner while Miss Dawson, 25, is seeing a man she met in a night club. **Morality** campaigners and family groups accused the women of making a mockery of motherhood.'
>
> from *The Daily Mail*
> 31 July 1998

Television soap operas and situation comedies try to reflect real-life dramas. In the popular soap *Friends*, Ross has to deal with the fact that his wife has left him for another woman and the couple are bringing up the baby he fathered. *Eastenders* shows the pressures Simon and Tony undergo as they try to get society to accept their relationship.

Weekend parents

Most children of separated parents still live with their mothers. If a father moves out of the family home to live with his gay partner, it means that the children may well be spending weekends with their father and his partner. This may raise concerns for the mother who may be anxious about how her children might be influenced, and for the father who may be worried about what his children might think. The children might themselves be confused about the changes in their lives.

Extra pressures

Gay partnership families have the added pressure of some people's prejudices and moral views as well as all the usual **pressures** that a family face. There is much argument about the wrongs and rights of 'gay families' but they exist and appear to be as likely to succeed as any other kind of family unit.

A gay man with his son and homosexual partner.

Extended families

An extended family is one which has extra relatives living with the **nuclear family**. These are usually grandparents but may also be other relatives such as aunts or uncles.

In Britain extended families were common until the 1950s. Afterwards new government policies enabled retired people to support themselves with pensions and other social benefits. They could afford to be independent.

It is now usual in Britain for old people to live on their own. However, when an elderly person is no longer able to look after themselves, their extended family sometimes offers to share their own home.

Other cultures

Many different cultures have settled in Britain since the 1950s. Some of these cultures believe that the extended family is the most responsible and natural way to live family life. In these cultures, when a couple marry they automatically live with the son's parents, and in time their children will become part of that family. The extended family can be seen most commonly today in families which have originated from Asian countries, such as China, India and Pakistan.

This extended family spans three generations.

The place of old people

An extended family is most commonly formed by a grandparent moving in and living with a **nuclear family**. When one grandparent dies and the remaining grandparent is no longer able to support themselves, it often happens that the **widowed** partner moves into the home of one of their married children.

Some families feel unable to offer a home to an elderly parent. An alternative place to live may be an old people's home, but the existence of such homes is controversial. Many people argue that it is morally wrong to put a parent into a home. Others argue that the **pressures** of modern life mean that it is often impossible for the family to care for an elderly parent. Different solutions suit different families.

Ageism

Many people feel that we no longer respect old people, the way we did in the past. They believe that today's culture encourages the view that old people are a burden. Some people believe that old people have nothing to offer because they are no longer earning a living and contributing to the country's economy.

Other cultures treat their elders as people with experience and wisdom, from whom younger people can learn. Previous generations in Britain mainly shared this attitude and it is only in recent times that prejudices against old people have developed. We now find our prejudices are being challenged by these more positive approaches to old age. These varying attitudes towards the elderly often influence how we treat family members when they become financially dependent.

Dependent relatives

Some families are extended out of choice, but in the UK most relatives living with a nuclear family are dependent. This means that they are unable to support themselves, either because of age, illness or financial hardship.

Living with a dependent relative can change the family dynamics and increase pressures on a family. It can be hard for the dependent relative to feel comfortable in someone else's home. Yet there are many advantages. We can learn a great deal from living with people of different age-groups, and an additional family member leads to a stronger family identity.

I know Grandad is deaf but he has the telly on so loud! Dad says we should understand but when Grandad falls asleep and snores through the best programmes it drives him nuts too! But I wouldn't change the situation for anything – I love Grandad.

My Mum's brother is ill and he's got no one to look after him, so Mum and Dad took him in. I feel sorry for him but life at home has changed. There's an atmosphere and Mum cries a lot. Dad goes out more. I feel guilty saying this, but I just wish Uncle Dave would die.

My Gran makes real chips. I love it now she's moved in with us because my Mum doesn't have time to cook properly every day, whereas Gran makes puddings and everything.

Foster families

A **foster** parent is someone who offers a home to a child on a temporary basis, while the child's own family sorts out their problems.

Is Your House a Happy House?

foster a child

RING SOCIAL SERVICES SOON!

Social Services

Social Services offers a payment to foster parents so that adults who wish to offer a home to a child, or children, in need can have the financial support to do so. But the money only covers the basic needs of the child, it is not a source of extra income. Social Services is an agency which acts as communicator and links the family, child and foster family.

Foster parents

Children who go into foster care may face an unsettling and distressing period of change. It could leave them feeling frightened and distrustful. This is one of the reasons why foster parents have to undergo interviews and assessments with Social Services before they are allowed to care for children – to make sure they understand the children's point of view. The interview process has recently become especially thorough since it was discovered that some fostered children had been **abused**.

People become foster parents for varying reasons. They may not be able to have or adopt children of their own, or they may wish to offer a home to a child in need, often alongside their own children.

Because foster families are temporary for the children concerned, the foster parents have to learn to handle situations that are often traumatic, emotional and painful. They must offer love but try not to get too attached to the children they care for.

CASE STUDY

Part 1

Marie, aged seven, lived with her single-parent Mum, Debbie. Debbie took drugs and found it difficult to earn enough money to support Marie and her drug habit. She started drug dealing but was eventually caught, convicted and sent to jail. Marie had no other relatives who were alive or known, so Social Services had to find her a foster family.

What's happened to Mummy? Where has she gone?

I don't want to live with someone else.

Where will I live?

Who's going to look after me?

They might not like me. I'm scared.

I might not like them.

CASE STUDY

Part 2

Don and Joan have two children of their own, Joe and Sara, and foster children on a regular basis. They **adopted** one of their foster children, Nathan, when he was ten years old. Now he is 16 and studying for his GCSEs at school. Social Services asked them to look after Marie while her Mum was in jail. When Marie first met them she found it hard, was hostile and would not talk. Eventually, after a week of treating her with care and understanding, Marie started to open up.

> I still miss Mum.

> Joan told me that my Mummy had made some mistakes because she was sad and that she was in prison. She's asked me if I want to visit her.

> I like Joe. He's Don and Joan's youngest. He's nine. He's got guinea pigs. Sara's cool. She lets me borrow her makeup. Don and Joan said maybe I can have a hamster.

> Mummy wrote me a long letter. It made me cry. I want to visit her but I'm scared.

> The best part of the day is when we cuddle up on the sofa and watch TV before bedtime. I wish Mummy could cuddle up with us.

CASE STUDY

Part 3

When she is released from prison Debbie must sort out her problems. Only then will Marie be allowed to return to her care. Meanwhile, Debbie will be able to visit Marie, and when Debbie has found somewhere to live, Marie will be able to stay with her Mum for the occasional weekend. This will gradually prepare everyone for the more permanent change to come.

During all these events new relationships have been formed; bonds and trust have been tested. The most vulnerable person in this situation is the child. How she is affected depends on many things. Will Debbie be able to stay away from drugs? Has Marie formed a strong bond to Don and Joan and their family? How will Debbie and Marie get on together now? Does Debbie resent interference from Social Services? Is she jealous of Marie's relationship with Don and Joan? Can Marie trust Debbie again?

CASE STUDY

Part 4

Marie has visited her Mum in jail, but they both always end up crying. Joan asked Social Services to stop the visits, so Debbie unwillingly agreed. Debbie has stopped taking drugs while in jail. She has had time to think about Marie and is determined to get her back. She knows that she must find a job and somewhere to live before Social Services will let Marie live with her again.

> I've got used to other kids coming and going. It doesn't change things between me and Mum and Dad. I think I'm lucky to have such great parents.

> I liked Marie. I don't mind Mum and Dad fostering. I think they're born to it! But I hate it when the kids go back to their parents. I mean, what are they going back to?

> Mum and Dad – that's Don and Joan – are great. They've always treated me like one of the family. I don't know if all foster parents are like them. Maybe I'm just lucky.

23

Adoptive parents

What are they?

Adoptive couples take in a child and treat him or her as their own. It is a step on from **fostering** because when a child is legally **adopted** it is placed in the permanent care of the adoptive parents.

How did it start?

In the 19th century some children's homes began to 'board out', or foster, younger children with 'approved' families. Sometimes these arrangements became permanent, although the arrangements had no official status.

In the UK campaigns for the legal recognition of adoption led to the foundation of adoption agencies in the 1920s. Later, the 1948 Children Act paved the way for adoption to become the main child care alternative to natural families.

Initially, it was mainly **illegitimate** babies who were adopted. This was at a time when having a child outside a marriage was seen as a sin. Illegitimate children were called **bastards**. Adoptive parents tended to be young married couples who could not have children of their own. So adopting a baby became a popular alternative to having your own children. In peak years one care agency was finding families for more than 300 infants a year.

Knowing the truth

It used to be a policy that children were not told they were adopted. Information about their real parents was confidential. Sometimes not even the adoptive parents were told the whole background of their new child. Since then a generation of adopted children have grown up and have spoken out about how this has affected them.

> 'I had to be totally determined in order to find out who my real parents were. Eventually I tracked my Mum down. She was 16 when she got pregnant and her parents made her put me in care. She told me my Dad was some lad she went to school with. We've become friends now. But we lost those years. We'll never get them back.'
>
> Nicola, aged 35

> 'I've never found out who my real parents were. My adoptive parents are great. It's not that I don't love them but I just want to know who I am. I've had all the love and support anyone could ask for but I can't get rid of the thought that my Mum might be out there, and why did she give me away?'
>
> Zak, aged 14

Modern policies

Modern thinking favours being as open and honest as possible with children and their adoptive parents. Knowing one's roots is seen as an essential part of becoming a secure and confident adult. Children are encouraged to think well of their birth parents and to try and understand the reasons behind their adoption.

Children are carefully matched with adoptive families and more placements are being found for children who are usually difficult to place, such as older children and those with special needs because of disabilities or histories of **abuse**.

1

I'm adopted. I'm happy but I'd really like to meet my real parents. What should I do?

Try to track them down. Contact an adoption agency. Find them.

2

OK, so now I know their names. So, I could stay happy but ignorant and try not to think about them or I could arrange to meet them and get involved again. What would you do?

3

Do nothing. Why stir it all up again? If they'd wanted you they would have looked for you by now.

Your real Mum and Dad are the ones who have cared for you and loved you all these years. Why mess up their lives now just out of curiosity.

Action For Children

NCH

Go for it. You'll never rest until you know the truth.

Why not get advice from these people?

Children's homes

Then...

In Victorian Britain poor people struggled to survive. Parents in need of support had no one to turn to. Often, children were abandoned and left to scavenge and beg on the streets. They were homeless. Others suffered the fate of prison-like institutions set up for orphans.

A few people were unable to turn a blind eye to their suffering. Some politicians fought for social reform. Charles Dickens wrote a novel based on the problem.

> 'The room in which the boys were fed, was a large stone hall, with a copper at one end: out of which the master, dressed in an apron for the purpose, and assisted by one or two women, ladled the gruel at meal-times.'
>
> from *Oliver Twist* by Charles Dickens first published in 1838

Others took action in the streets. The Reverend Stephenson was appalled by the deprivation of some children.

> 'Here were my poor little brothers and sisters sold to Hunger and the Devil. How could I be free of their blood if I did not try to save some of them?'
>
> Reverend Stephenson, founder of the first National Children's Home, 1869

And so children's homes were born. The most well known of these now are Barnardo's and the National Children's Home.

...and now

Large organizations where children were kept housed, clothed and fed were called **orphanages**. In Britain these no longer exist. Modern children's homes try to offer emotional support as well as the essentials for survival. Because of this they tend to be smaller. Some children stay in children's homes until they are old enough to look after themselves but many are **fostered** or **adopted**.

Planning for the future

Problems in some children's homes, foster homes and boarding schools led to a government decision to provide more protection for young people in **residential units**. Some adults take advantage of the vulnerable situation of young people in care, and a series of **abuse** scandals led to British government ministers setting aside £380 million in 1998 for children in care.

Frank Dobson, the Health Secretary for the British Labour government in 1998 said, 'We started from a recognition that if the whole system had failed these children, then the whole system had to be put right.'

Local authorities run many residential children's homes around Britain and are trying to change their image from that of institutions for the homeless to more caring family-style homes.

MEASURES TO IMPROVE CHILDREN'S LIVES IN CARE

- The creation of a group to provide a voice for children in care.
- Wider access to police checks on people working with youngsters.
- An extensive training programme for foster carers and staff of children's homes.

Other ideas to combat the wrongs inflicted upon children in care include appointing a Children's Commissioner who would be responsible for their welfare.

CHILDREN'S RIGHTS

The National Children's Home echoes the United Nations statement of Children's Rights:

We believe that:

- all children have the right to grow up in an environment which gives them protection from harm and where they feel safe and cared for
- everyone has potential to learn, grow and change and therefore we are committed to the strengths, resilience and personal resources of families
- our services should be sensitive to the **gender**, race, class, religion, culture and **sexual orientation** of the people who use them – and we work positively to achieve this
- everyone has the right to be respected
- everyone has the right to be heard
- discrimination should be challenged
- positive images of difference should be promoted.

'We are expecting a new arrival. Another girl to make our family complete. When she arrives there will be six children in all – and fourteen carers to look after them. We've tried to make this place as much like a family home as possible. We've used warm colours in the decoration and the bedrooms are simple but cheerful and practical.'

Head of a residential home

'The house mother where I'm in care is great. She listens and she tucks me in at night. She hasn't got the time to be like a real Mum. But then I wouldn't want anyone to be like my Mum.'

Cherolyn, aged 10

Supporting the family

It's tough being a parent

Bringing up children is probably the hardest and most important job many adults ever have to do. Being a parent is a demanding, 24-hours-a-day job. In an average week in the life of a child a parent will have had to use recognized skills in nursing, teaching, health and **nutrition**, **counselling**, **psychology** and entertainment. Yet there is no training and there are no career prospects!

To help make teenagers aware of the responsibilities of having children, childcare is now taught in many secondary schools. Students carry dolls around with them for three or four days to help them realize how hard it is to be a parent 24 hours a day. The dolls cry during the night and demand regular attention.

Help!

Many adults enter parenthood without really thinking about the consequences of having children. Most manage to be good enough parents and get by with the help and support of family, friends and neighbours.

But some people don't have natural support systems. They may not take to parenting as naturally as they thought. They may have problems in their lives. There are many reasons why a parent may not be able to cope.

● PARENTS REQUIRED ●

To look after two children not yet born. Must have strong constitution. The successful applicants will have
- a sense of humour
- endless patience
- and the ability to juggle.

You will be expected to go without sleep, mop up vomit, change dirty nappies, feed, clean, comfort, entertain and educate your offspring as well as provide an income, and be loving, supportive partners to each other and keep your home clean and tidy.

No pay. Lifelong contract.
Holidays and days off to be negotiated with relatives, neighbours and friends.

Those interested in having a life of their own need not apply.

Because parents are under so many **pressures**, agencies have been established to offer support to families who need it. How much they can help depends on the family's needs. No one can wave a magic wand and make everything wonderful but they can try to assist a family through difficult times.

Friendship families

These are families who offer support to other families. There are a variety of reasons for this. Usually it is to give the family of a sick or disabled child a well-earned rest. The child is gradually given increased contact time with their friendship family so that the child and family have bonded before spending time together.

Family nurses

The term 'family nurse' may soon become as familiar as family doctor. Health services are now extending their health care to providing family nurses who will work in communities to ensure families are getting the care and support they need. This British government policy recognizes that supporting the family in the community may help to improve **stress**-related health problems.

Sisters and brothers

Friends or enemies?

A sister or brother can be your greatest ally or your worst enemy, and can often be both at the same time. The relationships between brothers and sisters vary enormously.

> 'Ali and I were always close. Ali was always my protector. He'd look after me, stand up for me. He's married now and we don't see each other that often. When we do, it's great! Just like we've never been apart.'
>
> Sunita, aged 35

> 'I remember when Suzie was born. Dad used to put me in the pram with her and take us for a walk. Even then I hated her. When Dad wasn't looking, I'd try to kick her out. To be honest, I suppose I was jealous of her. But we've never really got on. I've seen her once in the last five years'.
>
> Amy, aged 23

Sibling rivalry

Many sisters and brothers compete for their parents' affections. This competitiveness causes jealousy and insecurity. The position in the family will often affect this. The first-born child may feel resentful of the intrusion of a new baby. A second-born may feel second best. These feelings may affect their relationship as they grow up.

Role play

Studies by **psychologists** have shown us that how we behave with our brothers and sisters in childhood often affects the way we relate to others as adults. Our position in the family is also a factor. Most of our experiences with our family show us how to live harmoniously with others, and to relate to others with reason and tolerance. But many people have problems, the roots of which lie in their childhoods.

CASE STUDY

Dennis was the eldest child of four – he had two sisters and a brother. He was often left in charge of the family and expected to do adult tasks beyond his years. When he grew up he was ambitious and did well in his career. However, his work started to suffer when he began to cover up mistakes and errors. Then he suffered a nervous breakdown. His **therapist** counselled him on his inability to accept he could be wrong. He talked about how as a child he didn't dare make mistakes because he was afraid that his brothers and sisters would suffer and his parents would blame him.

It's not all bad

Having someone to share your moans and groans with, being able to talk to someone who understands what you're going through, having someone who'll stand up for you in an argument, sharing

> 'Even though Mary and I live miles apart, we always know that if we really need help then we're there for each other. That's what family is about. Being there for each other.'
>
> Tim, aged 44

clothes, toys, books, secrets, games...these are some of the pleasures of having **siblings**. Many brothers and sisters who fight and bicker during childhood are merely like puppies play-fighting. They are using those closest to them to practise their **assertiveness** skills for adult life. Later on they become close friends.

The only child

There is a **stereotyped** image of only children – they are pampered and protected little adults, unable to communicate with other children in quite the same way as children from bigger families. But an only child is as likely to have a rewarding childhood experience as a child that grows up with **siblings**.

'The only thing I feel I missed out on by being an only child was all the squabbling! I always had plenty of friends, but at the end of the day they went home. And that's the way I liked it. Then I could spend time with Mum and Dad. Missed out? You must be joking!'

Chandra, aged 22

The relationship between siblings can be one of the closest an individual may experience.

Dysfunctional families

A **dysfunctional** family, or unhealthy family, is one that is damaged by poor relationships within it. In a healthy family system, every person in the family must be valued members. Each person should get their needs met on a fairly regular basis and in fairly regular doses.

Of course, errors and imbalances happen and these usually resolve themselves – but not in a dysfunctional family. The errors mount up. Children from a dysfunctional family may grow up to be disturbed adults.

What are the causes?

Stress is a common factor in dysfunctional families. Stress is the term given to **pressures** on people which make them anxious and worried. When parents are under stress their children usually suffer, too. It is hard for children to make allowances for parents who are cross or bad-tempered. Children usually think it is their fault. Usually stressful situations are temporary but long-term stress in an individual puts stress on the whole family.

People under stress often look for an escape route. Although this may give immediate comfort it may be the cause of more problems. There can be many forms of escape and any number employed at any one time:

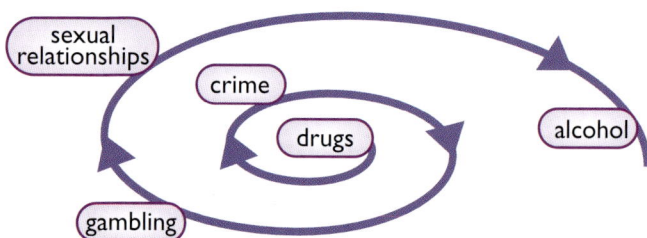

sexual relationships • crime • drugs • alcohol • gambling

What are the effects?

When someone is under the influence of an **intoxicant** they may not behave normally. Their feelings of failure or anger might be aggravated. This might lead to them becoming **abusive**. Usually, it is other members of the family who will be their victims. Hurting someone you love is a bit like hurting yourself. But when someone you love treats you badly this makes you think they don't love you.

A vicious circle

A child who has grown up in a dysfunctional family, and who has been unable to resolve their unhappy feelings, may become a parent who creates their own dysfunctional family. This is because they have not been able to learn healthy behaviour patterns from their family. They do not know any other way of living.

THE CAUSES OF STRESS

- unemployment
- lack of money
- difficulties at work
- relationship problems
- cramped living conditions
- not understanding children's behaviour
- illness

THE SIGNS OF STRESS

- feeling tired, listless or depressed a lot of the time
- being angry, short-tempered or tearful
- finding it hard to sleep
- feeling your heart beating faster than usual

Warning signs

Often, it is people outside the family who first notice signs of trouble in a family. A school may notice discipline problems in a child. Social Services might be called in by worried neighbours. The police may get involved because a crime is committed.

Sometimes, a distraught family member may themselves seek help. There are a variety of agencies who can provide help and support for families in trouble. Some are listed in this book on page 46. Unsatisfactory families can learn to be better and an unhealthy family can be healed. Often, the first step is admitting there is a problem and asking for help.

Healing ourselves

Being aware of how and why we behave the way we do can help us to help ourselves. Most agencies involved in helping families with problems identify what we all need to get from our family in order to be healthy, well-balanced individuals:

- love – the most essential need of all

- physical care – warmth, healthy meals, clean clothing and enough sleep
- respect – everyone deserves to be treated with courtesy
- praise – for the things we try to do, not just for what we achieve
- attention – making time to communicate with each other, listening and taking each other seriously
- stimulation – having enjoyable times together, like playing or sharing hobbies
- security – being there for each other and being able to trust one another.

If someone thinks their family, or themselves, have serious family problems then talking and sharing is the most important thing they can do. There are agencies listed at the back of this book which offer confidential support and guidance to anyone who needs it.

A child from a dysfunctional family is likely to repeat their parent's pattern of behaviour when they themselves become an adult.

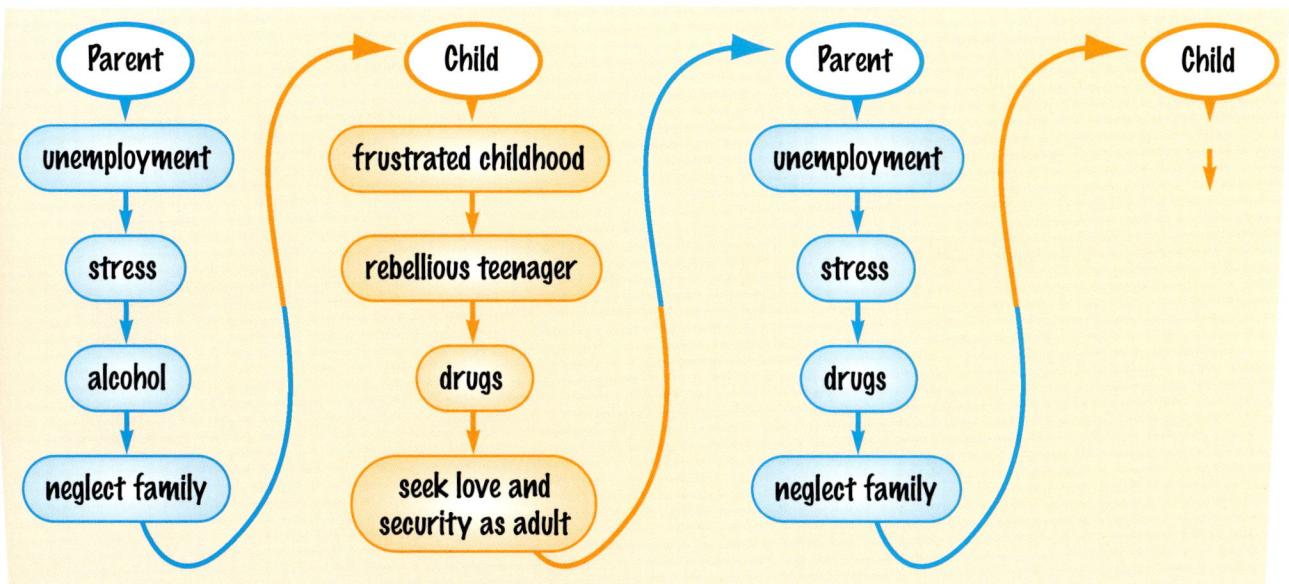

Parent → unemployment → stress → alcohol → neglect family

Child → frustrated childhood → rebellious teenager → drugs → seek love and security as adult

Parent → unemployment → stress → drugs → neglect family

Child

Violence in a family

Violence in a family can take different forms. Physical aggression is still the most common form of violence. It also includes bullying and sexual **abuse**.

Domestic violence

'Wife beating' is a common form of family violence. Most men are physically stronger than women and some men hit their partners under **stress** or during arguments. Many men are more likely to hit their partners when they are under the influence of alcohol.

Domestic violence represents 25 per cent of all recorded violent crime in Britain. Because women are unwilling to report their partners, it is suspected that there is far more violence than such statistics suggest. Domestic violence causes many families to break down and the break down of families has been blamed as a cause for violence in society in general.

JAMES'S STORY

James had to watch while his Dad systematically beat and raped his Mum. He was nine when he tried to intervene, and had the bruises to show for it. His father was eventually sent to prison for twelve months for the attacks on James and his Mum.

FACTS

Reports of domestic violence have increased more than any other type of violent crime over the last 15 years. In at least half the cases of domestic violence, children are also suffering abuse.

ASKING FOR HELP

If you suffer from violence talk to someone you know and trust. It will be the first step towards helping everyone. Help is available. Agencies are listed at the back of this book. Don't feel guilty. It is not your fault if your parents are violent. You need help and so do they.

How does it affect children?

Children may experience stress-related illnesses. Some may be very afraid or angry. They may lose confidence and feel they are to blame. They may become depressed and withdrawn. They may turn into bullies or become violent themselves.

Representative statistics on domestic violence are hard to establish as many violent crimes in the home go unreported.

Child abuse

Some children experience the pain of being beaten, humiliated, or sexually abused by their parents, or by other family members.

'My Dad told me that it was normal for him to have sex with me. Because he was my Dad, I had to believe him. He wants me to do all sorts of sexual things. I don't want my Dad to go to jail. I just want it to stop.'

Jo, aged 12

'My mother shouted at me practically all the time. Once she lashed out at me. She shook me violently and really frightened me. She would turn me out of the house in the middle of the night. Sometimes she kept me off school to do the housework. I'm really scared of her.'

Lin, aged 13

POSITIVE DISCIPLINE

If a child is 'told off' occasionally it does not mean the child is being abused! Positive discipline is required to bring up well-behaved children.

(See EPOCH on page 41).

FACT

An estimated 150–200 children a year die in England and Wales, following incidents of abuse or neglect. Thousands more suffer long-term emotional and psychological problems because of ill-treatment by their own parents or carers.

Types of child abuse

There are four main types of abuse.
PHYSICAL ABUSE: this includes hitting, shaking, squeezing, burning, biting, excessive force in feeding, changing or handling, poisoning, suffocating and drowning. Some studies show that more than one in four seven year-olds are hit with an object, such as a stick or belt.
EMOTIONAL ABUSE: this is when parents fail to show affection to their child. It includes bullying tactics such as threats, taunts, shouting and causing the child to lose confidence and self-esteem. Many emotionally abused children find it difficult to form trusting relationships later in life.
NEGLECT: this is when parents fail to provide the essential needs of their child, such as clothing, food and medical care. It also includes leaving young children to care for themselves. Although not violent in itself, it does inflict suffering on the child. A child under the age of five dies every week following abuse or neglect.
SEXUAL ABUSE: this is when a parent forces a child to take part in sexual activity to satisfy their own desires. The sexual abuse of children often includes additional violence.

How can we stop it?

More awareness, parent education and family support are all ways of helping parents avoid becoming violent. When a person is found to be violent they may discover that part of their treatment is to receive training on how to handle their anger. Many violent offenders have histories of violence against them, so positive steps towards breaking the cycle of violence is now seen as more effective than just punishment.

Serious illness, death and loss

All families have to cope with a serious illness or the death of a loved one at some time. Many of us will have to live through such difficult times while we are still growing up.

Illness

Reaction to serious illness involves many emotions. These are shown in this child's experience of her mother getting cancer:

- shock – the realization that a parent can be frail too 'Why won't she get up?'
- distress – because things aren't the same anymore 'I don't like Mum being ill! When will she get better?'
- worry – things seem out of control 'What are we going to do? Who will take me to football? How will Dad cope?'
- anger – because life is so unpredictable 'Why did this have to happen to us?'
- sorrow – feeling helpless and sad 'Will she die? I love her. She's in pain.'

As well as having to cope with these emotions, too, a partner has to carry on supporting the children and dealing with the extra practical demands. It can be a very **stressful** time for a family.

A sick or disabled child can place unintentional demands on the rest of the family. The parents may well have to devote a lot of time to caring for their child. This may mean that one of them has to give up work. The loss of earnings will affect the material well-being of the family

as well. Brothers and sisters may miss the attention of their parents and feel excluded from what is going on.

The serious ill health of a family member can bring a family together in their love and concern, but it can also pull it apart.

> ## HELP IS AVAILABLE
> Various support groups can help and advise children who have a relative who is ill. See the list of agencies at the back of this book.

Young carers

A young carer is anyone aged between 5 and 18 who takes a substantial role in caring for an adult or sibling who has physical or mental health problems. They may be caring for a parent, grandparent, brother, sister or other relation. The work may include helping with daily household tasks or personal care.

Young carers may be under **pressure** for different reasons:

- fear – they are frightened of asking for help in case the family is split up
- helplessness – no one seems to listen to them and they never feel they have done enough
- ilsolation – they may become isolated from school and social activities and from friends and family who don't understand their situation.

The carers
- *There are between 15,000–40,000 young carers in Britain*
- *average age is 12 years old*
- *61% are girls*
- *10% care for more than one person*
- *60% live in lone-parent families*
- *30% care for someone with mental health problems*
- *26% are missing school*
- *34% have some educational problems*

The cared for
- *61% are mothers*
- *17% are fathers*
- *17% are siblings*

Many young carers become strong and responsible adults, but it can be at the expense of their childhood.

Death...

GRANDPARENT: the death of a grandparent may well be the first experience of death we have. Sometimes we may feel that death is what happens to other people so it can be especially traumatic when our first experience of death is the death of someone so close to us.

PARENT OR CHILD: it may take a long time before the family can accept the death of a parent or child. Often, one family member may be hit harder than the others.

STILLBIRTH AND MISCARRIAGE: each year around 8000 babies in Britain are stillborn or die in **miscarriage**. Mourning the loss of a baby is important for parents because it is a recognition that the child was a part of the family's life, if only for a short time.

A mother dealt with her loss by writing to her dead baby:

'Your father was wonderful, never leaving me for a moment. After 17 hours, I felt you being born. I looked down: you were very still, but perfect. The nurse wrapped you in a shawl and let me cuddle you for a while. I didn't want to let you go.'

Bereavement is the imposed loss of someone you love, usually by death. It involves many complex emotions: shock, denial (can't believe it has happened), guilt, anger, bargaining and depression. Acceptance comes finally when you feel able to get on with your own life. You can help someone who is mourning the loss of a loved one by encouraging them to talk about their feelings. Most people who are grieving need a great deal of friendship and support before they finally come to terms with death. However, time does help the healing process. The bereaved person will eventually feel ready to carry on with their own life.

Teenagers

There is no particular age at which a child turns into an adult. It starts approximately at the age of 11 and finishes roughly at the age of 18.

Puberty

During this period, a child will start to experience changes in their body and their feelings. This is called puberty. It is a difficult time for human beings because there has to be an adjustment between who they were and who they are becoming. For the parent of a child going through puberty it can be just as bewildering, as their son or daughter starts to show changes in personality and becomes much more **assertive**.

Although many children grow into adults with no fuss, most experience conflicts of emotion, frustrations and feelings that are difficult to deal with.

When parents become a drag

Suddenly recognizing that your parents are not heroes but human beings can be difficult for a teenager. It can make you angry and blame them. What is actually happening is that you are realizing and having to come to terms with the fact that one day you will be an adult too.

Finding our own voice

Adolescence is a time when we start to assert ourselves. We won't do as we are told unless we agree with it. We question our parents instead of believing they know best. This usually causes arguments in families.

Did you see the dresses Mum bought us today? There's no way I'm ever going to wear one!

I don't think they realize we have grown up and don't want to wear matching clothe

Towards independence

Most teenagers, often between the ages of 16 and 18 will start to earn their own money, or go away to college or university. This is the beginning of their independence. Their new way of life may be their own choice and no longer dependent on what their parents want. This begins a period of change for the family which everyone has to adapt to.

Dangers for young adults

If a teenager leaves home before they are able to support themselves they may find difficulties in finding somewhere to live. Young homeless people are a very real problem in Britain today. Most of them have left home because they have fallen out with their parents, or suffered from neglect or **abuse**.

> 'Homelessness can be hell for young people, not only because of the conditions, but because it seems there is no way out.'
>
> Tony Blair,
> British Prime Minister

Sex, drugs and alcohol

Because they are turning into adults, it is natural for teenagers to want to experiment with adult pleasures. Many young people will become sexually active by the time they are 15. Most teenagers will try alcohol, and some may experiment with illegal drugs.

Young people can be vulnerable because they can be influenced by **peer group pressure** or try things without thinking about the consequences. Parents can find having teenagers a particularly worrying time because they may no longer be able to guide or control their children's behaviour.

Juvenile crime

The evidence shows that most young offenders will have had problems at home. They may have experienced inconsistent parenting, missed out on school, or been in care, unemployed or homeless. In Britain there are approximately seven million offences committed each year by 10–17 year-olds.

What makes a good parent?

Does it come naturally?

To many of us, certain caring and nurturing tasks are biologically natural. However, not everyone copes well with being a parent. There are other factors, such as your health, wealth, education, how you were parented and the age at which you become a parent, which will affect your parenting skills.

In the past, adults tended to get on with parenting, and did not question their abilities. Today, adults spend more time considering the likely problems of parenthood. They believe that if we are better parents, our children may become better adjusted adults.

> 'Modern parenthood is too demanding and complex a task to be performed well merely because we have all once been children.'
>
> Mia Kellner-Pringle,
> Director National Children's Bureau

Learning to be a good parent

Some organizations have been set up to teach parents their job, rather than rely on the fact that parenting is instinctive.

'Parent Network was founded in 1986 in response to the growing awareness that parents throughout Britain might benefit from support and education to help improve relationships with their children and enhance the well-being of the whole family.'

This was written by Dr Hilton Davis, the Consultant Psychologist at Guy's Hospital, London. He evaluated courses run by Parent Network and found that:

- 93% of parents felt more confident after completing the course
- 72% of parents observed significant improvement in their children's behaviour
- 95% of parents felt that they had gained new skills.

Most parents thought they were better able to understand and listen to their children and to deal with their problems.

Punishment

There is a lot of controversy about how to make a child behave well. Many methods which have long been used by parents are now being questioned. Some people's ideas of what makes a well-behaved child are other people's ideas of a repressed child who may become **delinquent** or **rebellious** later on.

Smacking

Five European countries have banned all physical punishment of children. Many people in other countries want to see smacking banned too. There is a great deal of argument over whether a smack can make violence seem acceptable to a child. Others believe that a smack is a safe way of persuading a child to behave.

EPOCH

EPOCH (End Physical Punishment of Children) is a national group in the UK which claims that smacking is a short-cut method of punishment with long-term ill effects. They give advice on how to bring up well-behaved children without resorting to hitting them. Their keys to good behaviour are founded on a belief in positive discipline – which builds on a child's desire to please and does not try to make children good by punishing them when they are naughty.

Quality time

When both parents are working, time is at a premium. The phrase 'quality time' is now often used for the limited time that some parents have with their children. The parents try to make the most of the time they have by giving their children full attention and doing special things with them.

Good enough

Feelings of not being a good parent have led to the phrase 'good enough'. This means that parents can only do so much as parents and should feel happy that they are being 'good enough' in raising their children to become stable adults.

Surrogate mothers

Some women are unable to have a baby. A controversial way of helping is through **surrogacy**. This is when a woman offers to provide her egg and womb so that others might be parents. Advanced technology has made this possible. However, there are many people who think it is wrong and that it should be illegal – especially if a childless couple pay a surrogate mother to have a baby for them.

Fathers

There are organizations that have been set up for fathers who feel that they suffer most when a marriage breaks up. Usually, the mother is awarded **custody** of the child and this has led to many fathers feeling forced to give up family life. These groups offer support to fathers to help them keep in contact with their children.

Teenage years can be difficult – it is a learning curve for parents as well as children.

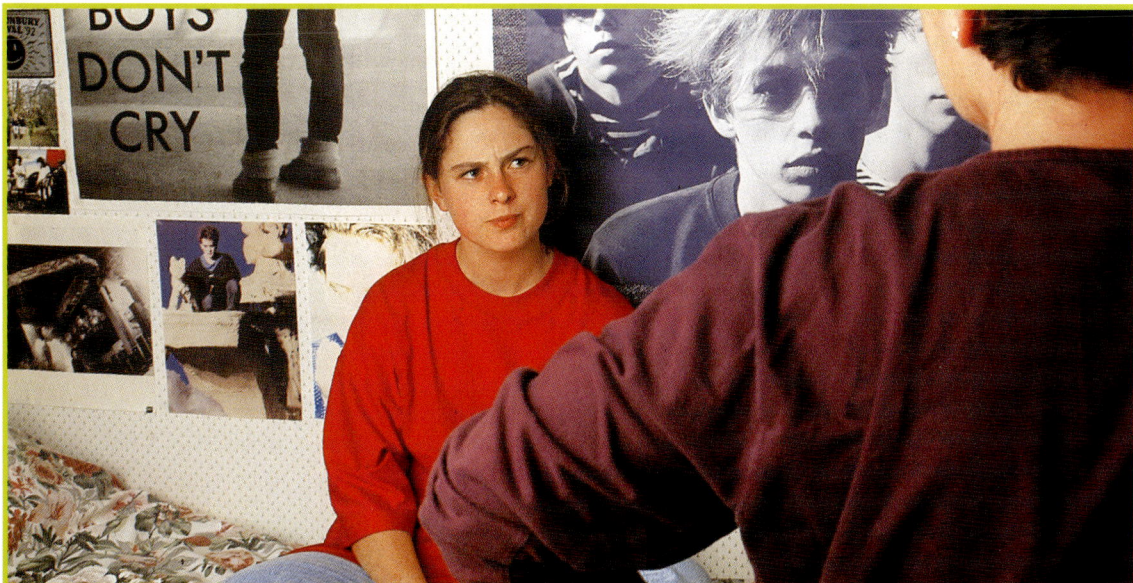

Families of the future?

On an Israeli Kibbutz, childcare is usually shared. A few adults look after all the children, who often live and sleep together.

At present families are undergoing major changes. There are many people who believe that family life is in danger and that we no longer value it. They point to the increase in one-parent families, the alarming divorce rate, and the fact that many people do not marry.

There are those who believe that we should return to traditional values and that our society is in danger unless we return to strong family units. They point to the increase in violence in our society and the way in which so many young people turn to drugs and alcohol.

But there are other views too. Is it realistic to return to the past? Should we not be considering alternative methods of having a stable and happy society?

Communes

Commune comes from the word 'communal'. A commune is a group of people who live together and share tasks, responsibilities and living space. All kinds of people live in a commune. A commune is usually based on an agreed ideal, religious or political view.

One place where communes have become successful alternatives to traditional family units is Israel, where a commune is called a Kibbutz. A Kibbutz is a group of various individuals and families who share all their property and earnings. They also share the work load and the care of the children and dependent relatives.

Influences on the family

Projected figures for the western world suggest that there will be certain changes to the population which will affect family life. For example, there will be a growth in the numbers of old and very old people, and there is a trend towards smaller families with just one or two children.

The British government is keen to promote more traditional family values, such as two-parent families and a more responsible attitude to caring for children. Other influences are to do with our beliefs and attitudes. Some religious beliefs which influenced family life in the past have been rejected. In today's **multicultural** society there is a wider range of beliefs and influences which affect family life.

What do we want?

The emphasis in modern life is on the individual. These days everyone is aware of their rights. There are children's rights and human rights. There are even animal rights. People are more **assertive** and aware of their needs and wishes. Family life in the future may reflect more strongly the importance of the individual.

Responsibility to others

Human beings will always need one another. In 1997 the number of births in England alone was 641,142. But can we make couples who no longer love each other stay together for the sake of the children? Do children want that? Can we change our views about partnerships so that when we join with another person we no longer necessarily expect to stay together for life? As we improve our personal and social skills can we improve our tolerance and understanding of others, so that we are more likely to stay in partnerships for longer?

Fantasy families

Everyone hopes that life will change for the better. There have always been problems in family life although the nature of the problems may change. The pressures on families today may be many and varied, but there is also much to be gained from family life.

We just need to understand that a 'happy family' simply means a family that works well.

I'm Helene Patel. These are Rosie and Rea Irani, my children from a previous marriage.

My name is Ken, I live with Steve now. My ex-wife Clare is married to Pete. We have two kids, Simon and Nathan.

I'm Guy's partner

I'm Tara. My ex is Guy. Now I'm pregnant with Ali's baby.

My name is John Smith. My wife is Helene Patel. This is my first son James Smith and my second son Ravi Smith-Patel.

I'm Hanna, this is Xi and our baby Josh.

Hi. We're George and Esther and this is our grand daughter, Jodie.

Glossary

abuse to treat badly, taking unfair advantage of another person

adoption the act of taking on as your own. This usually applies to adults who wish to take on a child and treat him or her as their own.

adultery having sex with someone when you are married to or **co-habiting** with another person

ageism a prejudice against people because of their age

ancestor a past relative (descendant) of a mother or father

assertiveness standing up for your rights and opinions

bastard an abusive term originally used to describe a child born out of marriage

children's commissioner an adult who is employed by the government to take care of children's issues and ensure that children are protected

coffer a strong box that used to be used to hold valuables

co-habit to live in a sexual partnership with someone without legally marrying

contraception the practice by couples of using a device to prevent pregnancy

controversy a conflict of ideas about a subject which people feel strongly about

counselling taking advice and talking to a qualified professional in order to solve problems or overcome them

custody the legal care of another

delinquent a young offender who has broken the law

discriminate to treat others differently, often unpleasantly, because they are different from you

donor someone who gives something to another person

dowry the property brought to a marriage by the woman

dysfunctional describing something abnormal

foster to care for and nurture a child in the absence of legal carers such as parents

gender a person's sex, either female or male

heterosexual attracted sexually to someone of the opposite sex

homosexual attracted sexually to someone of the same sex

illegitimate the out-dated term given to a child born out of marriage

inseminate to place sperm into a woman's womb

intoxicant a substance that alters and affects the mind, such as alcohol or drugs

legal guardian someone who is given the legal responsibility to bring up a child or ensure that a child is cared for

lesbian a female homosexual

marital relationships this refers to sexual intercourse between married people

media the organizations through which news is communicated, such as TV, newspapers and magazines

miscarriage the loss of a child who is born prematurely and unable to survive independently

morality a code of how to behave in a good or right way

multicultural being of more than one culture, race or religion

nuclear family a family that consists of parents and their children

nutrition eating what is healthy and good for the body and mind to develop and grow

orphanage a home for children who have no other carers

peer group pressure pressure from a group of people of the same age and interests

prejudice disliking someone or something because of what or who they are, without any particular reason for doing so

pressure a feeling of being overburdened or in difficulty and feeling unable to cope

prosperous having wealth and material well-being

psychologist a professionally qualified person who studies the way the mind works and helps people with mental or emotional problems

rebellious not accepting others' behaviour and lifestyles as the only way to live, and living or behaving in a deliberately different way

reconstituted put back together again

repressed having feelings and emotions that you are unable to express, which then create problems

residential home/unit a place where children go to live and where they are cared for by professional people when they have no other responsible guardians

sexual orientation a sexual preference, either for those of the same sex or to those of the opposite sex

sibling a brother or sister

spouse a sexual partner, usually a married partner

stereotype to have a fixed idea about a person or thing, giving them qualities that you associate with that person or thing, whether they have them or not

stillbirth when a child is born dead, who otherwise could have lived outside the mother's womb

stress an intense pressure or tension which can cause upsetting or out-of-character reactions

surrogacy providing the womb to have a baby for another woman who cannot have her own children

therapist a professional person who is qualified to listen and advise those who have problems

Universal Declaration of Human Rights a list of what human beings should be allowed to do as part of their right to be living. This was made to try and stop people causing suffering by abusing others

welfare state the country where a welfare system is put into practice

welfare system the government group that takes responsibility for people's means of survival and health

widowed someone whose partner has died

WW1, WW2 abbreviations for World War One and World War Two

Contacts and helplines

CARERS NATIONAL ASSOCIATION

20-25 Glasshouse Yard, London SW6 1EE
Provides information for young carers

THE PARENT NETWORK

11 Cranmer Street, London, SW9 EJ
0171 735 1214

CHILDLINE

Freepost 1111, London, N1 OBR
0800 1111 – Children can write or phone if they
have a problem of any kind

EPOCH

77 Holloway Road, London, N7 8JZ
0171 700 0627 – Helps develop non-violent
methods of bringing up children

FAMILIES NEED FATHERS

BM Families, London, WC1N 3XX
081 886 0970

Scotland contact:

Parents Forever Scotland
0333 352034 – Helps parents keep in contact with
their children after separation

GINGERBREAD

16–17 Clerkenwell Close, London, EC1R OAA
0171 336 8183 – Self-help group for single parents

HOME-START UK

2 Salisbury Road, Leicester, LE1 7QR
0116 2339955 – Helps families under stress,
in their homes

**MEET A MUM ASSOCIATION
(MAMA)**

26 Avenue Road, London SE25 4DX
0181 771 5595 – Support for women who
experience problems after having a baby

**NATIONAL COUNCIL FOR ONE
PARENT FAMILIES**

255 Kentish Town Road, London NW5 2LX
0171 267 1361 – Advises single parents on benefits
and rights

**NCH (National Childrens Home)
ACTION FOR CHILDREN**

85 Highbury Park, London, N5 1UD
0171 226 2033 – Offers a variety of services to
families and young people

**NSPCC (National Society for the
Prevention of Cruelty to Children)
NATIONAL CENTRE**

42 Curtain Road, London, EC2A 3NH
0171 825 2500
Child Protection Helpline: *0800 800 500*

**NATIONAL STEPFAMILY
ASSOCIATION**

72 Willesden Lane, London, NW6 7TA
0171 372 0844

**NEWPIN (New Parent and
Infant Network)**

Sutherland House, 35 Sutherland Square, Walworth
Road, London SE17 3EE
171 703 6326 – Support and training for parents of
new babies

PARENT ADVICE CENTRE

Franklyn House, Brunswick Street, Belfast
BT2 7GE *01232 238800* – Guidance and counselling
for, parents and young people with family difficulties

PARENTLINE

Endway House, Endway, Hadleigh, SS7 2AN, *01702
559900* – Parents who need help and support

RELATE

Herbert Gray College, Little Church Street, Rugby,
CV21 3AP, *01788 573241* – Provides counselling and
support for anyone with relationship problems.

In Australia, use the following contacts:

**AUSTRALIAN INSTITUTE OF FAMILY
STUDIES**

300 Queen Street, Melbourne, Victoria 3000
(03) 9214 7888 http://www.aifs.org.au

KIDS HELPLINE

1800 551800 – Freecall for advice and support

REACH OUT

http://www.reachout.asn.au

Further reading

Non Fiction

Adolescence
Nicholas Tucker
Wayland Press, *Human Development*
series, 1990

Barnado's
Diane Church
Heinemann, *Taking Action* series, 1997

Child Abuse
Angela Park
Franklin Watts, 1988

Contemporary Moral Issues
Joe Jenkins
Heinemann, 1998

Disabled People
Peter White
Franklin Watts, 1988

Disabilities and Equality

Marriage and Divorce

Separation and Divorce

Single and Lone Parents

*Too Old – Who Says – Our Ageing
   Generation*

Violence in the Family

What are Children's Rights?
Craig Donnellan
Independence, *Issues for the Nineties*
series, 1996

Divorce
Liz Friedrich,
Franklin Watts, 1988

Family and Friends
John Coleman
Wayland Press, 1990

Moods and Feelings
John Coleman
Wayland Press, 1990

Rights in the Home
E Haughton and P Clarke
Franklin Watts, 1997

Shelter
Katrina Dunbar
Heinemann, *Taking Action* series, 1997

Step Families
Elizabeth Hodder
Gloucester Press, 1990

Rights of Women
Mandy Wharton
Franklin Watts, 1988

Index